HIGH PRAISE

**SONGS FROM SCRIPTURE
IN 4 PART HARMONY**

COMPILED BY
JONATHAN LYLE

HAROLD SHAW PUBLISHERS
WHEATON, ILLINOIS 60187

Scripture quotations, unless otherwise noted,
are from the King James Version.

Address all inquiries to Harold Shaw Publishers,
Box 567, Wheaton, IL 60187.

ISBN 0-87788-771-3

Library of Congress Catalog Card Number 77-78753

Printed in the United States of America.

Third Printing, March 1982

Foreword

The infant church was accustomed to the practice of singing the Psalms. Music and church history books tell us that the singing of Psalms and other Scriptures has never disappeared from the church. During the first part of this century, in addition to the serious and sophisticated singing of Scripture anthems by church choirs, there was some interest shown in setting Scripture to more spontaneous melodies to be sung by congregations.

It is this setting of Scripture passages to brighter, folk-type melodies that is becoming increasingly popular today.

Some have observed that most special visitations of the Holy Spirit through the centuries have been characterized by new songs. If that is true, then the present era of renewal and revival is no exception.

These songs are representative of church renewal music in the last few years—highly singable and enjoyable music which communicates on various levels of Christian experience.

Special thanks and appreciation are due here to Rich Sutliff, who arranged most of the music, his wife Shirley, who transcribed and checked all the arrangements at the piano, and Phil White, who then edited the entire songbook. Every attempt has been made to arrange the songs well within the vocal range of the average congregation. While this benefits the singers, it may create difficulties for the guitarist who has to play in an unfamiliar key. In such cases, alternate chords in a more playable key are added in parentheses.

It is the desire of the compiler, arranger, and publisher that this collection in four part harmony, become valuable to you in church gatherings, choral arrangements, youth meetings, church camp programs, home study groups, family singing, and in your personal devotions.

Since the purpose of these songs is to encourage you in the worship of God, you may find it helpful to sing the same song over several times, and so gain more meaning each time, through meditation on the words and their significance. Avoid switching quickly from song to song. After you have learned several of these songs you will find that you have memorized several Scripture passages! This is one of the "fringe benefits" of singing the Scriptures.

Thus we encourage you to "address one another in psalms and hymns and spiritual songs, singing and making melody to the Lord with all your heart." (Eph. 5:19) It is doubtful if there is any more enjoyable way of hiding God's Word in your heart, or of praising your Maker and Lord.

—Jon Lyle

1 God is Not a Man

Numbers 23:19, 20 Unknown

G C Cm G
3
God is not a man, that He should lie; nei-ther the
3
D7 G
son of man, that He should re - pent: hath He said and
C C°7 G D7
shall He not do it? or hath He spo - ken, shall He
G G7 C D7/C
not make it good? Be - hold, I have re - ceived com -
G A9 A7
mand - ment to bless: and He hath blessed; and I can -

D7 D7#5 G C Cm
not re - verse it. For God is not a man, that He should
G D7 G
lie; nei-ther the son of man, that He should re - pent.

2 Hear, O Israel

Deuteronomy 6:4, 5

Don Brynteson

F Dm Bb G9 C6 C7 Am C7
Hear, O Is - ra - el: the Lord our God is one Lord: And thou shalt

Dm Gm G9 C F Dm Bb G9
love the Lord thy God with all thine heart, and with all thy soul, and with

C Am Gm7 Dm Gm C7 Bb6/F F
all thy might. Hear, O Is - ra - el: the Lord our God is one Lord.

3 I Will Proclaim the Greatness of the Lord

Deuteronomy 32:3, 4, 6, 8-10 TLB Jim Levin

F Bb F Dm C
1. I will pro-claim the great-ness of the Lord. How glo-ri-
2. Many years a-go God di-vid-ed up the world, He di-vided it
3. For Is-ra-el was spec-ial to the Lord; His per-son-
F Bb C7 Bb F Am7 Dm
rit.
ous He is! Ev-'ry-thing He does is just and fair:
in-to nations. To each He gave an an-gel strong,
al pos-session. He guarded them a-long the way;
C7 F C7 F Dm Am
a tempo
CHORUS
He is faith-ful with-out sin.
but to Is-rael He gave none. Is not God your Fa-ther? Has He
the ap-ple of His eye.
Dm Am Dm Am Bb F C7
not es-tab-lished you, and has He not made you strong?
made you strong?

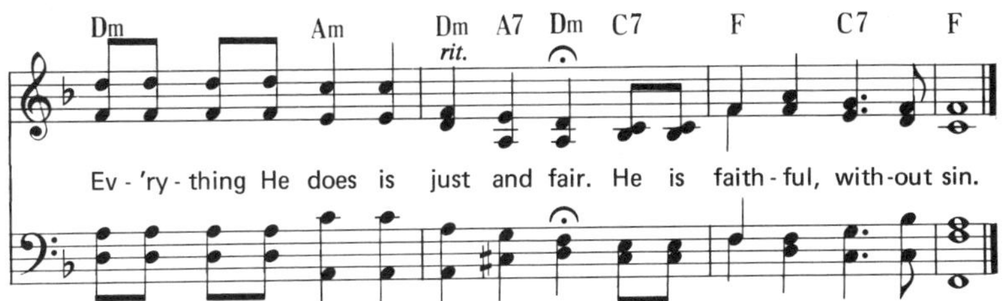
Dm Am Dm A7 Dm C7 F C7 F
rit.
Ev - 'ry - thing He does is just and fair. He is faith - ful, with-out sin.

4 The Lord Will not Forsake His People

1 Samuel 12: 22 AMP.

Jonathan Lyle

D G D Bm A7 1 D

The Lord will not for- sake His peo-ple for His great name's sake:

2 D D7 G D G

sake: For it has pleased Him to make you a peo - ple for Him-

D G D E7 A7

self; for it has pleased Him to make you a peo - ple for Him-self. The

melody

D G D E7 A7 D

Lord will not for - sake His peo-ple for His great name's sake.

5 Thine, O Lord, is the Greatness

1 Chronicles 29:11-13

Delinda Bishop

Bb (A) Eb (D) F (E) F9 (E9)
Thine, O Lord, is the great - ness; Thine, O Lord, is the
Bb (A) D (C#) D7 (C#7) Gm (F#m)
pow - er; Thine, O Lord, is the glo - ry, the vic - to -
C7 (B7) F (E) Bb (A)
ry, and the maj - es - ty: for all that is in the hea-ven and
Bb7 (A7) Eb (D) F (E)
earth is Thine; Thine is the king - dom, O Lord, and
Bb (A) Eb (D) F (E) Bb (A)
Thou art ex - alt - ed as head a - bove all. Both

F (E)
Bb (A)
F (E)
riches and hon - or come of Thee, and Thou reign - est o - ver
Bb (A)
D (C#)
D7 (C#7)
Gm (F#m)
all; and in Thy hand is pow - er and might; and in Thine
D (C#)
Gm (F#m)
F (E)
C7 (B7)
hand it is to make great, and to give strength un - to
F (E)
Bb (A)
Eb (D)
F (E)
all. There - fore, our God, we thank Thee, we thank Thee, we
Bb (A)
Eb (D)
Bb (A)
F (E)
Bb (A)
thank Thee, and praise Thy glo - ri - ous name.

6 My Glory and the Lifter of my Head

Psalm 3:3, 4 — Mae McAlister

C G7
My glo-ry, and the lift-er of my head; My glo-ry and the
G7 C C7 F
lift-er of my head; And thou, O Lord, art a shield to me my
G G7 C Fine G
glo-ry and the lift-er of my head. I cried un-to the Lord
C G C G
with my voice; I cried un-to the Lord with my voice; I cried un-to the
G7 C D G7 D. S. al fine
Lord with my voice, and He heard me out of His ho-ly hill, My

7 As for God, His Way is Perfect

Psalm 18:30, 31

Debbie Milbradt

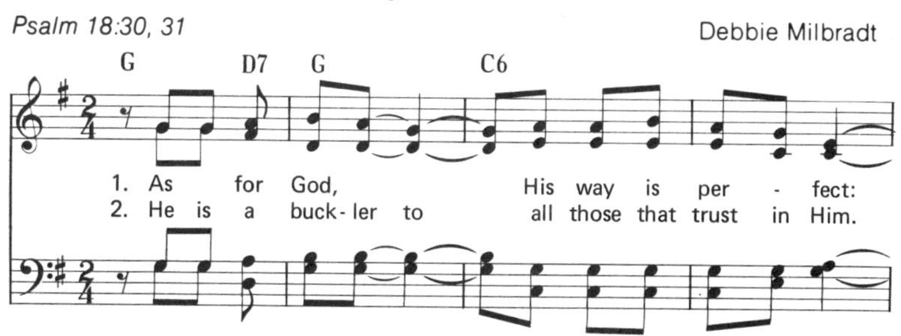
G D7 G C6
1. As for God, His way is per - fect:
2. He is a buck - ler to all those that trust in Him.

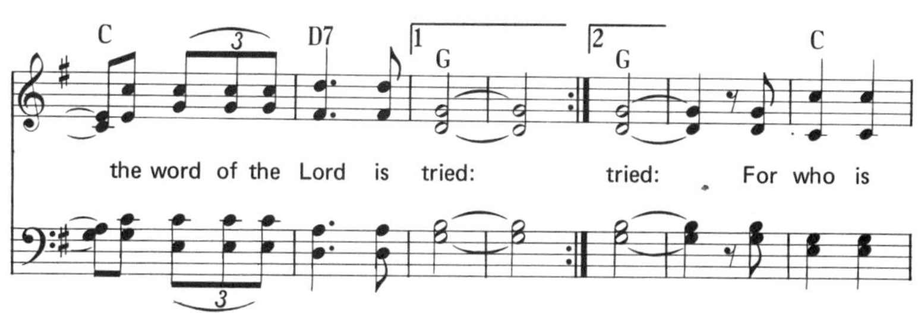
C D7 1 G 2 G C
3
3
the word of the Lord is tried: tried: For who is

D G7 C Am7 A9 D D7 G
God save the Lord? or who is a rock save our God? As for

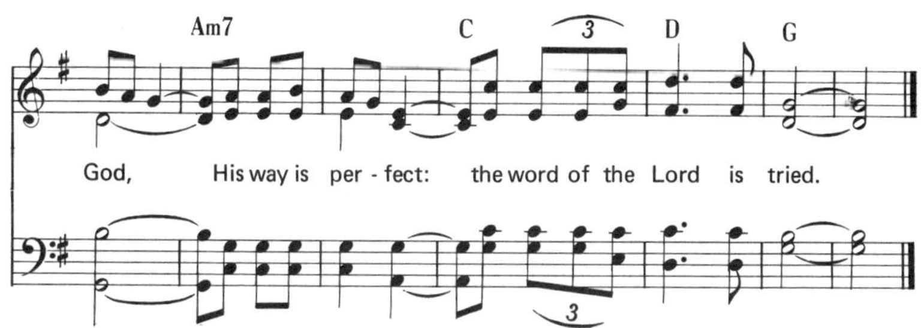
Am7 C D G
3
3
God, His way is per - fect: the word of the Lord is tried.

8 The Heavens Declare the Glory of God

Psalm 19:1-4a

Joe Friberg

F C7 F Dm
The heav-ens de - clare the glo - ry of God; and the
B♭ Gm C9 F Fine F C7 F
fir - ma-ment show-eth His hand - i - work. Day un - to day
Dm B♭ G7 C9 F
ut - ter - eth speech, and night un - to night show-eth knowl-edge.
Women F
There is no speech nor lan - guage, their voice is not heard,
Piano
B♭7
Piano
D. C. al fine
Their line is gone out to the end of the world.
Men

9 Unto Thee, O Lord

Psalm 25:1-5, 7, 9, 14, 20 verses 1, 3 Charles Monroe

1. Un - to Thee, O Lord (Un - to thee, O Lord), do I lift up my soul.
2. Yea, let none that wait (Yea, let none that wait), on Thee be a - shamed.
3. Show me Thy ways (Show me Thy ways), Thy ways, O Lord.
4. For Thou art the God (For Thou art the God), of my sal - va - tion.
5. Re mem - ber not (Re - mem - ber not) the sins of my youth.
6. The meek will He guide (The meek will He guide), will He guide in judg-ment.
7. The se - cret of the Lord (The se - cret of the Lord) is with them that fear Him.
8. O keep my soul (O keep my soul) and de - liv - er me.
Un - to Thee, O Lord (Un - to Thee, O Lord), do I lift up my soul.
Yea, let none that wait (Yea, let none that wait) on Thee be a - shamed.
Teach me Thy paths (Teach me thy paths), Thy paths, O Lord.
For Thou art the God (For Thou art the God) of my sal - va - tion.
Re - mem - ber not (Re - mem - ber not) the sins of my youth.
The meek will He guide (The meek will He guide), will he guide in judgment.
The se - cret of the Lord (The se - cret of the Lord) is with them that fear Him.
O keep my soul (O keep my soul) and de - liv - er me.
CHORUS
O my God, I trust in Thee: Let me
not be a - shamed, let not mine en - e - mies tri - umph o - ver me.

10 One Thing Have I Desired

Psalm 27:4, 5 Unknown

F C B♭ F
One thing have I de - sired of the Lord, that will I seek
C F C B♭ F
af - ter; that I may dwell in the house of the Lord all the
C7 F F7 B♭ F
days of my life, To be - hold the beau-ty of the Lord,
C7 B♭ B♭m6 F F7 F
Fine
and to in - quire in His tem - ple. To be - ple.
F C B♭ B♭m6 F
For in the time of trou - ble He shall hide me in His pa-

C F C B♭ B♭m6 F
vil - lion: in the se-cret of His ta - ber-na - cle shall He
C F F7 D. S. al fine
hide me; He shall set me up up - on a rock. To be -

11 Wait on the Lord

Psalm 27:14

Bob and Kathy Wright

G D7 G C Am7
Wait on the Lord: be of good cour - age, and
G Em Em6 D7(sus) D7 G B7 Em
He shall strength-en thine heart. Wait on the Lord,
C Am7 G D7 G
wait on the Lord: wait I say, on the Lord.

12 I will Extol Thee, O Lord

Psalm 30:1, 2 Charles Monroe

I will ex- tol Thee, O Lord; for Thou hast lift - ed me up,
and hast not made my foes to re - joice o - ver me. O Lord my
God, I cried un - to Thee, and Thou hast healed me,
and Thou hast healed me. I will ex-tol Thee, O Lord; for Thou hast
lift - ed me up, and hast not made my foes to re - joice o - ver me.

13 The Lord is My Light

Psalm 27:1

Pauline Michael Mills

Bb(A)
Eb(D)
Bb(A)
The Lord is my light and my sal- va - tion; whom shall I
F7 (E7)
Bb(A)
F(E)
fear ? whom shall I fear? The Lord is my fear ? Whom shall I
Bb(A)
Fine
Gb7 (F7)
Bb(A)
fear ? The Lord is the strength, the strength of my life. Of
Gb(F)
F7 (E)
D. S. al Fine
whom, then, shall I be a - fraid ? The Lord is my

14 The Steps of a Good Man

Psalm 37:23, 24
Fred Zweifel
F F7 B♭ F
The steps of a good man are or - dered by the Lord. The
G C F
steps of a good man are or - dered by the Lord. The steps of a
F7 B♭ F C
good man are or - dered by the Lord: and He de - light - eth in his
F B♭ F G
way. Though he fall, he shall not be cast down; though he
C C7 F F7
fall he shall not be cast down. The steps of a good man are

Bb F C7 F
or-dered by the Lord: and the Lord up-holds him with His hand.

15 Delight Thyself Also in the Lord

Psalm 37:4, 5

Peter Dahlberg

Eb (D) Ab (G) Bb7 (A7) Eb (D)

De - light thy self al - so in the Lord; and He shall

Ab (G) Bb7 (A7) Eb (D) Eb7 (D7) Ab (G) Bb7 (A7)

give thee the de - sires of thine heart. Com - mit thy way un - to the

Eb (D) Cm (Bm) Fm (Em) Bb (A) Bb7 (A7) Eb (D)

Lord; trust al - so in Him; and He shall

Bb7 (A7) Eb (D) Cm (Bm) Gm (F#m) Ab (G) Bb7 (A7) Eb (D)

bring it to pass; and He shall bring it to pass.

16 I Waited Patiently for the Lord

Psalm 40:1-3 NASB Jonathan Lyle

Bb(A) F(E) Bb(A)
I wait - ed pa - tient - ly for the Lord, and He in -
Eb maj7(Dmaj7) Ebm(Dm) Bb(A) Gm(F#m)
clined to me, and heard my cry. He brought me up out of the
D(C#) Gm(F#m) D7(C#7) Gm(F#m) F7(E7)
pit of de - struc - tion, out of the mir - y clay. And He
Bb(A) Eb(D) Bb(A) F7sus(E7sus) F7(E7) Bb(A)
set my feet up - on a rock, mak - ing my foot - steps firm. And He
Eb(D) Bb(A) F7sus(E7sus) F7(E7) Bb(A)
set my feet up - on a rock, mak - ing my foot - steps firm. And He

E♭(D) B♭(A) C9 (B9) F7 (E7)
put a new song in my mouth, a song of praise to our God.
B♭(A) F (E) B♭(A) B° (A♯°) F7 (E7) B♭(A)
Man - y will see and fear, and will trust in the Lord.

17 Give unto the Lord

Psalm 29:1, 2

Fred Zweifel

C C7 F G

Give un - to the Lord, O ye might - y, Give un - to the

G7 C G7 C C7 F

Lord glo - ry and strength Give un - to the Lord the glo - ry

C Dm G G7 C

due His name; wor - ship the Lord in the beau - ty of ho - li-ness.

18 As the Hart Panteth after the Water Brooks

Psalm 42:1, 2; Isaiah 44:3 Unknown

C Cdim Dm
As the hart pant-eth af - ter the wa - ter brooks, so
Dm7 G G9 G7 C
pant-eth my soul af-ter Thee, O God. My soul thirst-eth for God,
C7 F C F G7
for the liv-ing God: when shall I come and ap - pear be-fore
C Cdim Dm
God? For I will pour wa - ter on him that is thirst - y, and
Dm7 G G9 C
floods up - on the dry ground: I will pour out my Spir - it

C7 F C F G C
up - on thy seed, and my bless-ing up - on thine off - spring.

19 My Soul, Wait Thou Only upon God

Psalm 62:5, 6

Anna Edson

My soul, wait thou on - ly up - on God; for my ex - pec - ta - tion is from Him. He on - ly is my rock and my sal - va - tion: He is my de - fense; I shall not be moved. My soul, wait thou on - ly up - on God.

20 God is our Refuge

Psalm 46:1, 2

Don Brynteson

F
C7
God is our re - fuge and strength. God is our re - fuge and
F
F7
Bb
strength, a ver - y pres - ent help in trou - ble. God is our
F
C7
F
C7
F
re - fuge and strength. There-fore will not we fear, though the
3
C7
Gm/C
earth be re - moved. there - fore will not we fear though the
C7
3
F
earth be re - moved, and though the moun-tains be car -

F7 3 B♭ Gm7 F C7 F
ried in-to the sea, God is our re- fuge and and strength.
3

21 Great is the Lord

Psalm 48:1, 2 Robert Ewing

Great is the Lord, and great-ly to be praised in the cit-y
of our God, in the moun-tain of His ho-li-ness. Beau-ti-ful for
sit-u a-tion, the joy of the whole earth, is mount
Zi-on, on the sides of the north, the cit-y of the great King.

22 I Will Sing of the Mercies

Psalm 89:1

James H. Filmore

D
I will sing of the mer-cies of the Lord for ev- er: I will
A7
D
sing, I will sing. I will sing of the mer- cies of the
A7
D
Fine
Lord for ev - er: I will sing of the mer-cies of the Lord.
D7
G
D
A7
With my mouth will I make known Thy faith - ful-ness, Thy
D
G
D
faith - ful-ness. With my mouth will I make known

A
E7
A7
D
D. S. al fine
thy faith - ful-ness to all gen - er - a - tions. I will

23 I Will Praise Thee

Psalm 86:12, 13

Charles Monroe

F7 (E7) Bb(A) F7 (E7)

I will praise Thee, O Lord my God, with all my heart,

Bb (A) Eb(D)

with all my heart: and I will glo - ri - fy Thy name for ev - er-

Bb(A) Eb(D) F7 (E7) Bb(A) Bb7(A7) Eb(D) Bb(A)

Fine

more, with all my heart. For great is thy mer-cy toward me: and

C7 (B7) F7(E7) C(B) F7(E7)

D. S. al fine

Thou hast de - liv -ered my soul from the low-est hell. I will

24 He that Dwelleth in the Secret Place

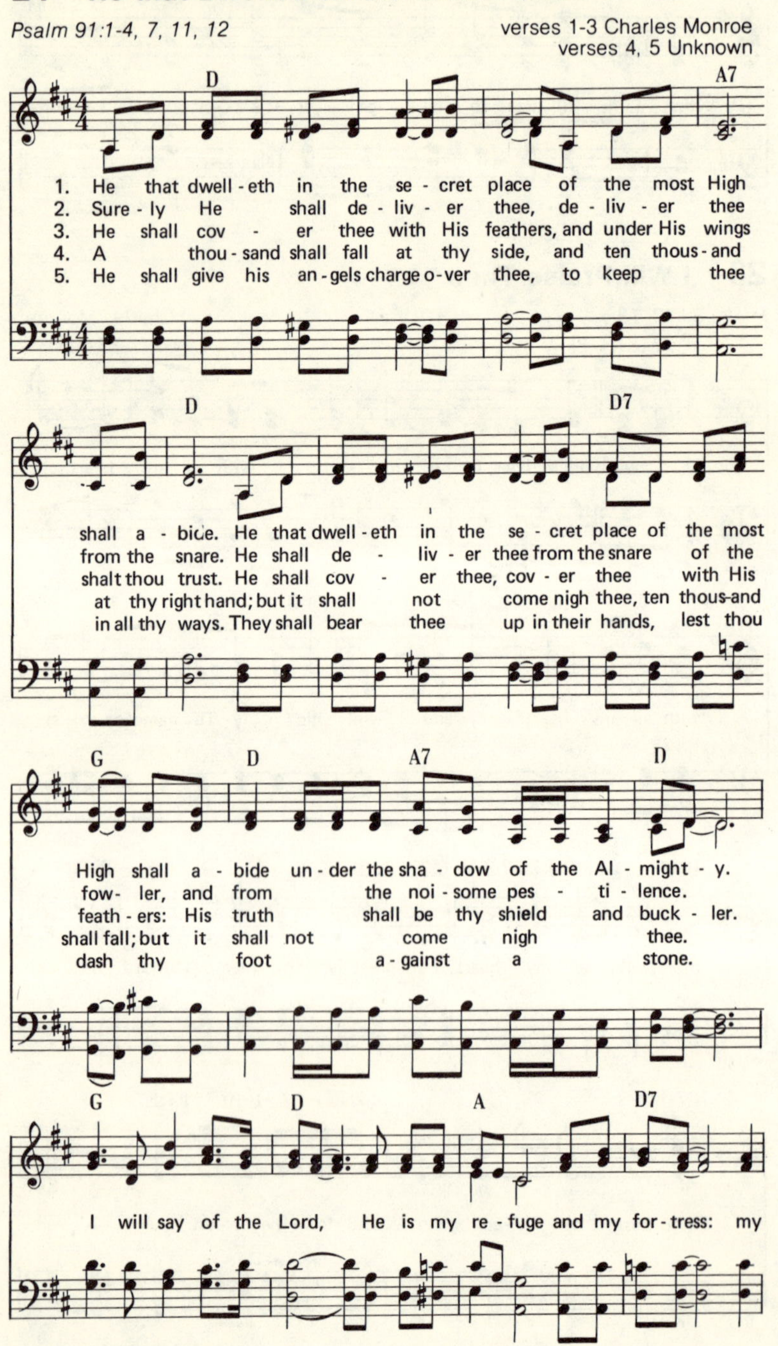

Psalm 91:1-4, 7, 11, 12
verses 1-3 Charles Monroe
verses 4, 5 Unknown
D A7
1. He that dwell - eth in the se - cret place of the most High
2. Sure - ly He shall de - liv - er thee, de - liv - er thee
3. He shall cov - er thee with His feathers, and under His wings
4. A thou - sand shall fall at thy side, and ten thous - and
5. He shall give his an - gels charge o - ver thee, to keep thee
D D7
shall a - bide. He that dwell - eth in the se - cret place of the most
from the snare. He shall de - liv - er thee from the snare of the
shalt thou trust. He shall cov - er thee, cov - er thee with His
at thy right hand; but it shall not come nigh thee, ten thous-and
in all thy ways. They shall bear thee up in their hands, lest thou
G D A7 D
High shall a - bide un - der the sha - dow of the Al - might - y.
fow- ler, and from the noi - some pes - ti - lence.
feath - ers: His truth shall be thy shield and buck - ler.
shall fall; but it shall not come nigh thee.
dash thy foot a - gainst a stone.
G D A D7
I will say of the Lord, He is my re - fuge and my for - tress: my

G D A7 D
God; in Him will I trust. He is my re - fuge and my for - tress.

25 Be Still and Know that I am God

Psalm 46:10

Jim Levin

D Bm G A7 D A Bm
Be still, and know that I am God. Be still, and know that

Em7 A7 G A7 D C♯dim Bm
I am God: I will be ex - alt - ed a - mong the hea - then,

G A7 D A7 D
I will be ex - alt - ed in the earth. Be still, and

Bm G A7 D Bm Em A7 D
know that I am God. Be still, and know that I am God.

26 Let the Beauty of Our God

Psalm 90:1, 2, 12, 14-17

Lucille Levin

D
Em7 A7
1. Lord, Thou hast been our dwell - ing place in all time. Be -
2. So teach us, Lord, to num - ber all our days,
3. Make us glad un - to the days thou hast af - flicted us,
Em/A
A7
D
fore the moun - tains were brought forth or formed, e'en from
that we may ap - ply our hearts to wis - dom. O
and the years where - in we have seen e - vil. O
Em A E7
ev - er - last - ing un - to ev - er - last - ing, Thou
sat - is - fy us ear - ly with Thy mer - cy; that we may re -
let Thy work ap - pear un - to Thy ser - vants, and Thy glo - ry
A7
D
O Lord, art God.
joice all our days. And let the beau - ty of our
be un - to their child - ren.
A7
God be up - on us. And let the beau - ty of our God be up -

D
D7
on us. And let the beau - ty of our God be up -
G
D
A7
D
on us; and es - tab - lish Thou the work of our hands, O Lord.

27 His Name is as Ointment Poured Forth

Song of Solomon 1:3 A. Cadman

G C G D
His name is as oint - ment poured forth: Je - sus,

D7 G D G C
Je - sus, Je - sus, Je - sus. His name is as

B D7 G D G
oint-ment poured forth. His name is as oint-ment poured forth.

28 Thy Lovingkindness

Psalm 63:3, 4 Unknown

Women:
D
A7
1. Thy lov - ing - kind - ness is
2. I lift my hands up
Men:
1. Thy lov - ing - kind - ness is bet - ter than life.
2. I lift my hands up in thy name.
Em
A7
bet - ter than life
in thy name.
Thy lov - ing - kind - ness
I lift my hands up
Thy lov - ing - kind - ness is bet - ter than
I lift my hands up in thy
D
D
D7
is bet - ter than life.
in thy name.
My lips shall praise Thee.
My lips shall praise Thee.
life.
name.
My lips shall praise Thee. Thus will I
My lips shall praise Thee. Thus will I
G
D
A7
D
Thus will I bless Thee: I will lift up my hands in thy name.
Thus will I bless Thee: I will lift up my hands in thy name.
bless Thee: I will lift up my hands in thy name.
bless Thee: I will lift up my hands in thy name.

29 For Thou art Great

Psalm 86:10-12

Public Domain

C Cmaj7 C Dm G7
For Thou art great, and do - est won-drous things: For
C G7
Thou art God a-lone. Teach me Thy way, O Lord; I will
C Cmaj7 C7 F
walk in Thy truth: u - nite my heart to fear Thy name.
C G7 F
I will praise Thee, O Lord my God, with all my heart:
Fm C G C
and I will glo - ri - fy Thy name for ev - er - more.
3
3

30 From the Rising of the Sun

Psalm 113:3, 1, 2 Unknown

Eb(D)
From the ris - ing of the sun to the go-ing down
Bb7 (A)
1
Eb(D) Ab(G) Eb(D)
of the same the Lord's name is to be praised.
2
Eb(D)
Ab(G)
Eb(D)
G (F#)
praised. Praise ye the Lord. Praise Him, O ye ser-vants of the Lord,
Ab(G)
Bb7 (A)
Eb (D)
praise the name of the Lord. Bless - ed be the
Ab(G)
Eb(D)
G(F#) Ab(G)
Bb7(A)
Eb(D)
name of the Lord, From this time forth and for ev - er - more.

31 This is the Day

Psalm 118:24

Maori Folk Tune

Eb(D) Bb7(A7) Eb(D) Bb7(A7) Eb(D) Bb(A)
This is the day, this is the day that the Lord hath
made, that the Lord hath made; We will re- joice, we will re-
Eb(D) Eb7(D7) Ab(G)
joice and be glad in it, and be glad in it. This is the
Eb7(D)Bb(A7)Eb7(D7) Ab(G) Eb(D) Bb(A) Eb(D)
day that the Lord hath made; we will re- joice and be glad in it.
Bb7(A7)Eb(D) Bb7(A7)Eb(D) Ab(G)Eb(D) Bb7(A7) Eb(D)
This is the day, this is the day that the Lord hath made.

32 If Thou, O Lord, Shouldest Mark Iniquities

Psalm 130:3, 4

Unknown

F Bb F
If Thou O Lord, shouldest mark in - i - qui -ties,
C F
who shall stand? who shall stand? If Thou, O Lord shouldest
Bb F Bb F C7 F
mark in - i - qui-ties, O Lord, who shall stand? But there is for-
C7 F
give - ness with Thee, but there is for-give - ness with Thee, but
F7 Bb F C7 F
there is for-give-ness with Thee, that Thou mayest be feared.

33 Behold! Bless Ye the Lord

Psalm 134 Janet Cameron

Em B7 Em Em B7 Em
Be - hold, bless ye the Lord. Be - hold, bless ye the Lord,

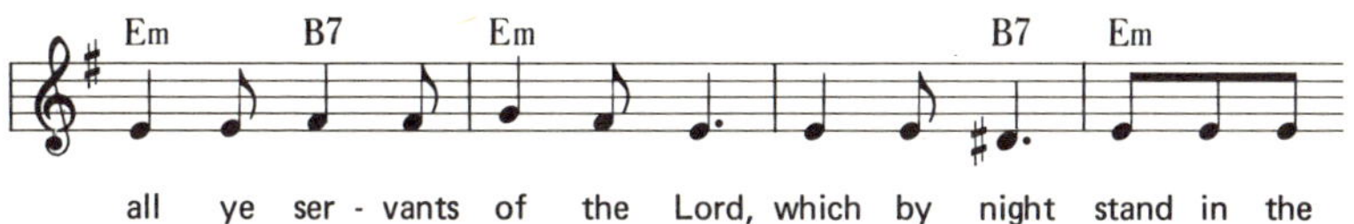
Em B7 Em B7 Em
all ye ser - vants of the Lord, which by night stand in the

B7 Em B7 Em
house of the Lord. Lift up your hands in the sanc - tu - ar - y and

B7 Em B7 Em
bless the Lord. The Lord that made hea - ven and earth

B7 Em B7 Em
Fine
bless thee out of Zi - on. Be - hold, bless ye the Lord.

*Sung as a round between men and women - (↓) - indicates start of second part.

34 Come, Bless the Lord

Psalm 134:1, 2 Unknown

D A7 D
Come bless the Lord,
Come bless the Lord, all ye ser - vants of the
A
all ye ser - vants of the Lord, which stand by
Lord, which stand by night
D A7
night in the house of the Lord.
in the house of the Lord. Lift up your
D D7 G
Lift up your hands in the ho - ly place,
hands in the ho - ly place, and bless the
D A D G D
and bless the Lord, and bless the Lord.
Lord, and bless the Lord.

35 Cause Me to Hear

Psalm 143:8-11, 6

Rosalie Monroe

D E Em A A7 D
Cause me to hear Thy lov - ing - kind - ness in the morn - ing;
Bm7 A D D E Em
for in Thee do I trust: Cause me to know the way where -
A7 D Bm A7 D Fine
in I should walk for I lift up my soul un - to Thee.
D7 G A A7 D Bm G E E7 A G
De - liv - er me, O Lord. Teach me to do Thy will. Quick- en
A A7 D Bm Em A7 D D.C. al fine
me, O Lord. I stretch forth my hands un – to Thee.

36 Praise Ye the Lord!

Psalm 150
Rita Kelligan
G C G
Praise ye the Lord. Praise God in His sanc - tu - ar - y:
C G A7 D
Praise Him in the fir - ma - ment of His pow'r.
G C G G D G
Praise Him for His might - y acts: Praise Him ac - cord - ing,
C G D G D
praise Him ac - cord - ing to His ex - cel - lent
G D G
great - ness. Praise Him with the sound of the trum - pet:

D
G
C
Praise Him with the psal - tery and harp. Praise Him with the
A7
D
A7
tim - brel and dance: Praise Him with stringed in - stru - ments and
D
D7
G
C
G
or - gans. Praise Him up - on the loud cym - bals:
3
Praise Him up - on the high sound - ing cym - bals. Let eve - ry
D7
G
G7
C
E♭7
G
D
G
thing that hath breath praise the Lord. Praise ye the Lord!

37 This is My Beloved

Song of Solomon 5:16 Delinda Bishop

G C D G

This is my Be - lov - ed, and this is my friend. He is

C A D
al - to-geth - er love-ly, my Be - lov - ed and my Friend.

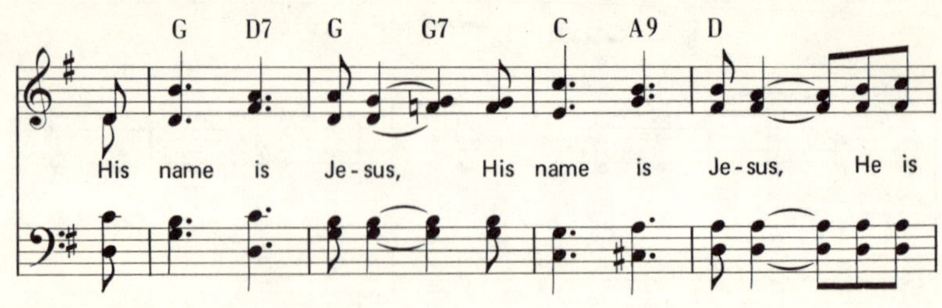

G D7 G G7 C A9 D
His name is Je - sus, His name is Je - sus, He is

G C G D7 G
al - to-geth - er love-ly, my Be - lov - ed and my Friend.

38 I See the Lord

Isaiah 6:1, 3 Anonymous

F Bb F C7
I see the Lord. I see the Lord; He is high and lift - ed

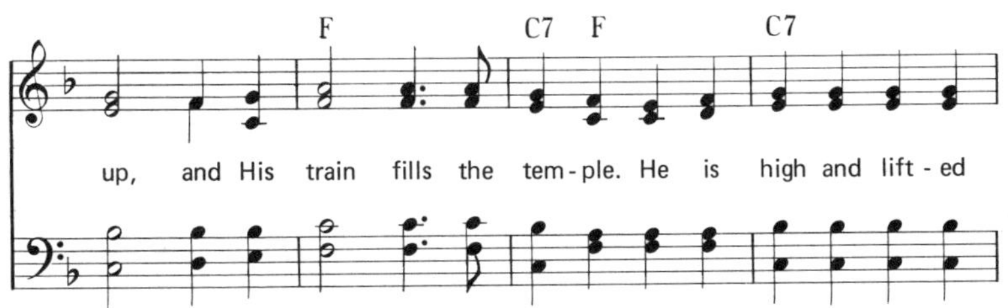

F C7 F C7
up, and His train fills the tem - ple. He is high and lift - ed

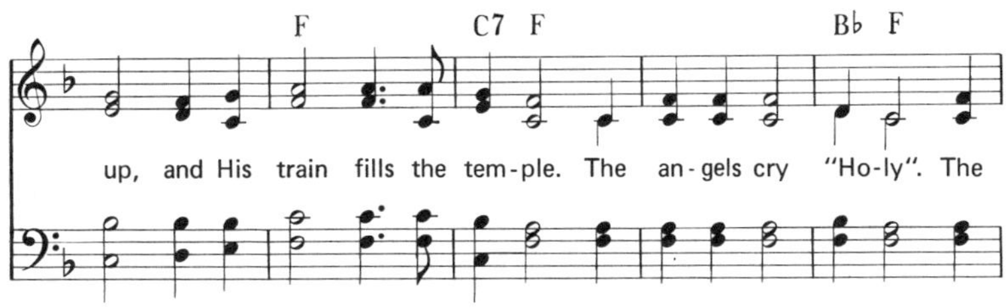

F C7 F Bb F
up, and His train fills the tem - ple. The an - gels cry "Ho - ly". The

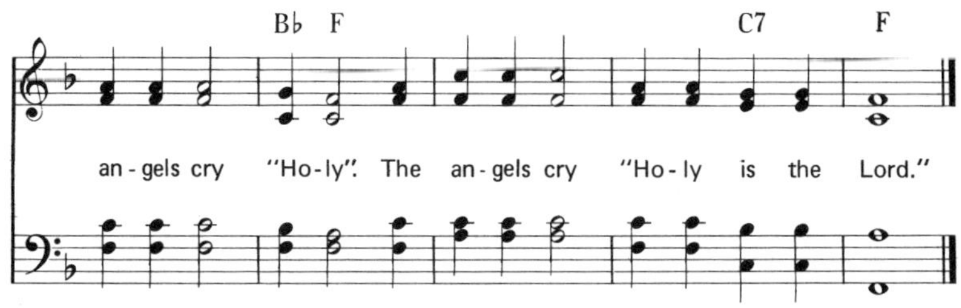

Bb F C7 F
an - gels cry "Ho - ly". The an - gels cry "Ho - ly is the Lord."

39 Therefore with Joy

Isaiah 12:3, 4 Unknown

Bb (A)
There-fore with joy shall ye draw wa - ter out of the
D(C#) Eb (D) Bb (A)
wells of sal - va - tion. And in that day shall ye
F (E) F7 (E7) Bb (A)
say, "Praise the Lord." There-fore with joy shall ye draw
D (C#) Eb (D)
wa - ter out of the wells of sal - va - tion. And in that
F(E) Eb(D) F(E) F7(E7) Bb(A)
day shall ye say, "Praise the Lord."

40 Thou wilt Keep Him in Perfect Peace

Isaiah 26:3

Dave Peterson

C Dm7 G C F
Thou wilt keep him in per - fect peace, whose mind is
G C F G Em A7
stayed on Thee. Thou wilt keep him in per- fect peace, whose
Dm7 G7 C C7 F G
mind is stayed on Thee. Be - cause he trust - eth in
C Am G7 C C
Thee: be - cause he trust - eth in Thee: Thou wilt
Dm7 G C F G C
keep him in per - fect peace, whose mind is stayed on Thee.

41 Therefore the Redeemed of the Lord

Isaiah 51:11 Ruth Lake

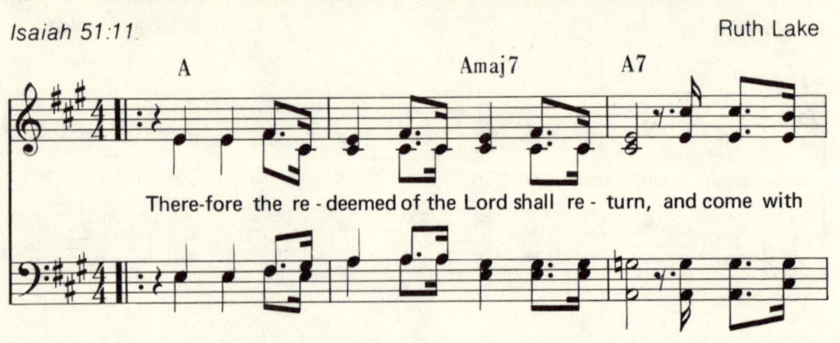
A
Amaj7
A7
There-fore the re - deemed of the Lord shall re - turn, and come with

D
A
F#m
sing - ing un - to Zi - on; and ev - er - last - ing joy shall

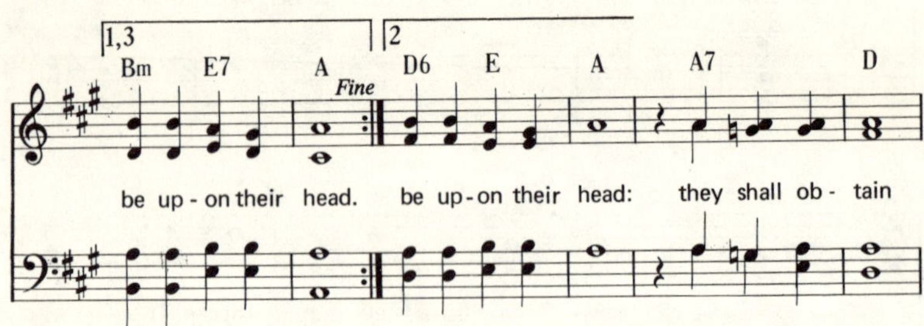
1,3
2
Bm
E7
A
Fine
D6
E
A
A7
D
be up - on their head. be up - on their head: they shall ob - tain

A
B7
E7
D. C. al Fine
glad - ness and joy; and sor - row and mourn - ing shall flee a - way.

42 Obey My Voice

Jeremiah 7:23
Sheilagh Nowacki
Eb (D) Gm(F#m) Eb(D) Ab(G) Bb (A) Eb(D) Gm (F#m)
O - bey my voice, and I will be your God, and ye shall be my
Cm7/F(Bm7/E) Bb7(A7) Eb(D) Gm(F#m) Ab (G) Bb(A)
peo - ple: and walk in all the ways that I've com-mand-ed you, that
Eb(D) Gm(F#m) Ab (C) Fm (Em) Db (A) Eb(D)
it may be well with you, and I will be your God. O - bey my
Gm(F#m) Ab (G) Bb (A) Eb (D) Cm (Bm) (G6) (A7) Ab6 Bb7 Eb (D)
voice, and I will be your God, and ye shall be my peo - ple.

43 Ah Lord God!

Jeremiah 32:17

John Rea

Ab(G)
Db(C)
Eb(D) Ab(G)
Ah Lord God! Ah Lord God! be hold, Thou hast made

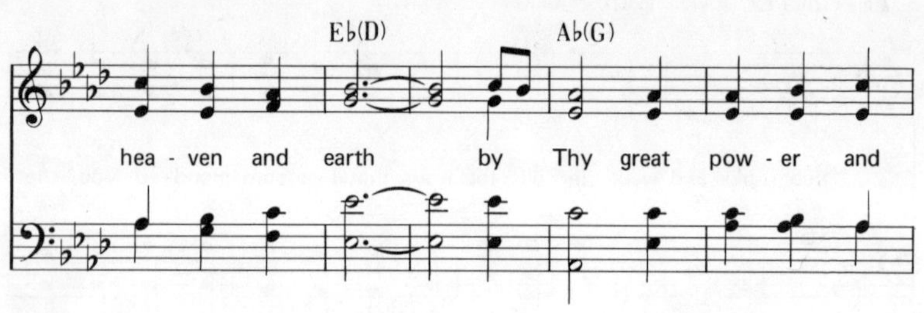
Eb(D)
Ab(G)
hea - ven and earth by Thy great pow - er and

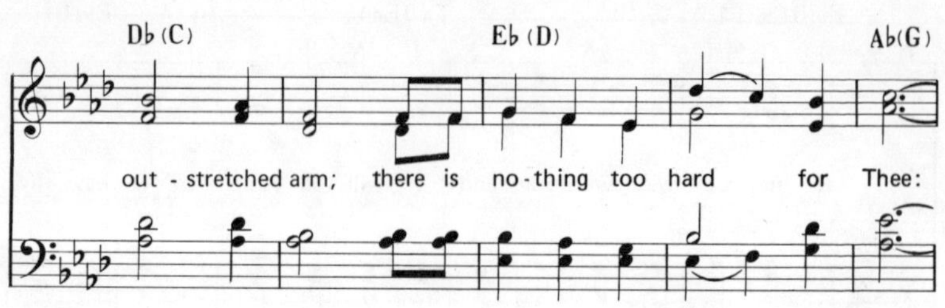
Db(C)
Eb (D)
Ab(G)
out - stretched arm; there is no - thing too hard for Thee:

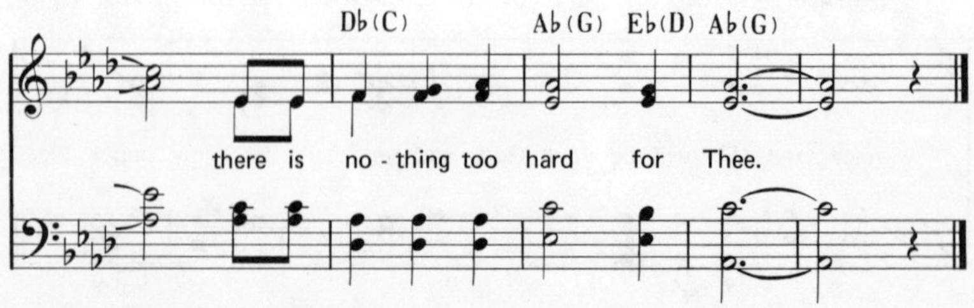
Db(C)
Ab(G) Eb(D) Ab(G)
there is no - thing too hard for Thee.

44 Let Us Know

Hosea 6:3

Elaine Hull

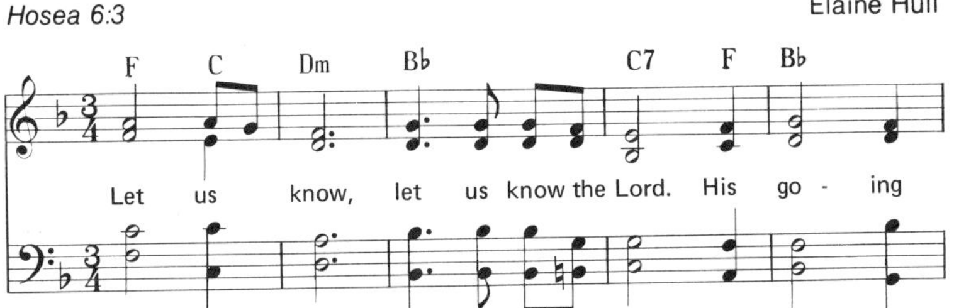
F C Dm B♭ C7 F B♭
Let us know, let us know the Lord. His go - ing

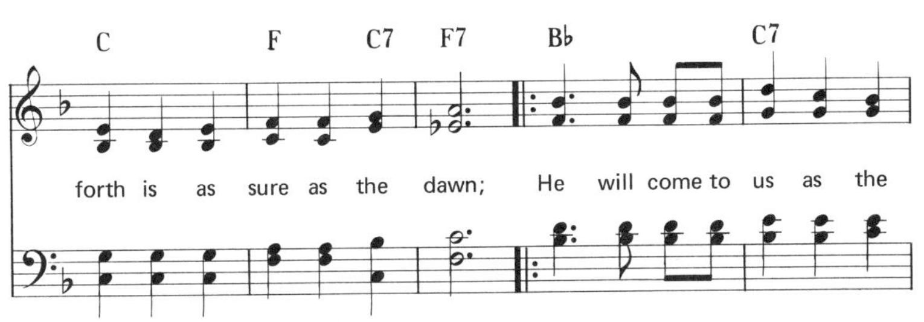
C F C7 F7 B♭ C7
forth is as sure as the dawn; He will come to us as the

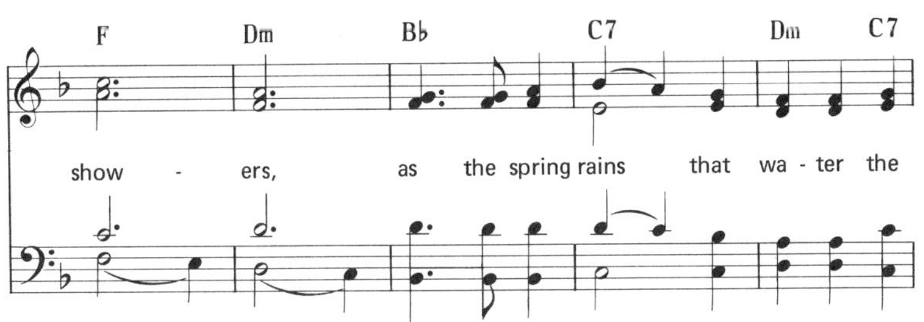
F Dm B♭ C7 Dm C7
show - ers, as the spring rains that wa - ter the

1 2
F F C Dm Gm C7 F
earth. earth. Let us know, Let us know the Lord.

45 Seek Ye First

Matthew 6:33, 4:4; 7:7; 11:28; Luke 9:23

verse 1 Karen Lafferty
verses 2-5 Unknown

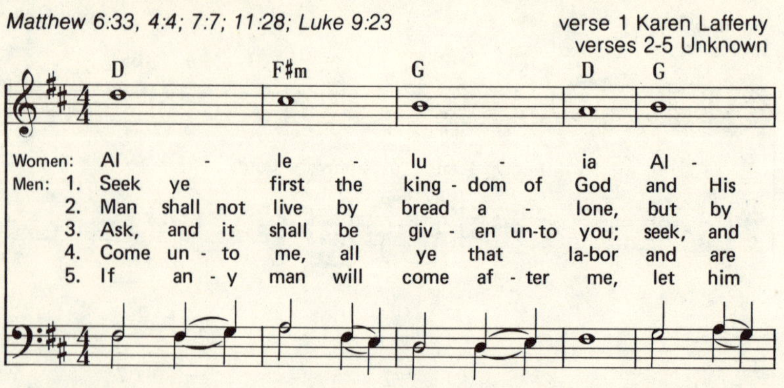
D F#m G D G
Women: Al - le - lu - ia Al -
Men: 1. Seek ye first the king - dom of God and His
2. Man shall not live by bread a - lone, but by
3. Ask, and it shall be giv - en un-to you; seek, and
4. Come un - to me, all ye that la-bor and are
5. If an - y man will come af - ter me, let him

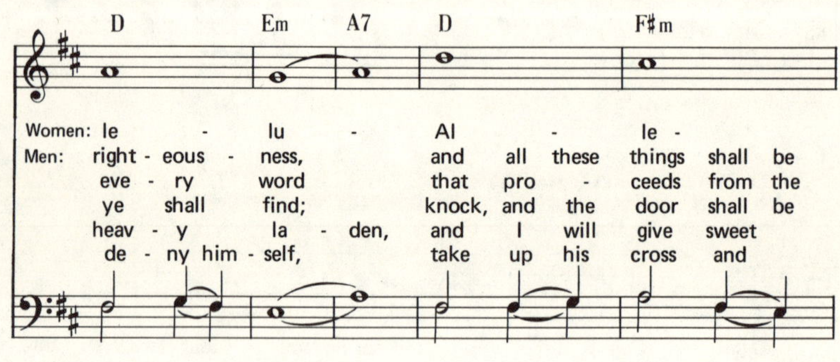
D Em A7 D F#m
Women: le - lu - Al - le -
Men: right - eous - ness, and all these things shall be
eve - ry word that pro - ceeds from the
ye shall find; knock, and the door shall be
heav - y la - den, and I will give sweet
de - ny him - self, take up his cross and

G D G D A7 D
Women: lu - ia Al - le - lu - ia.
Men: add - ed un - to you. Al - le - lu, al - le - lu - ia.
mouth of God. Al - le - lu, al - le - lu - ia.
o - pened un - to you. Al - le - lu, al - le - lu - ia.
rest un - to your souls. Al - le - lu, al - le - lu - ia.
dai - ly fol - low me. Al - le - lu, al - le - lu - ia.

 Verses 2-5 are not part of the song as originally written. Their origin is unknown.

46 In Him was Life

John 1:4, 11, 12

Unknown

C
C7
F
1. He came un - to his own, and his own re - ceived him not,
2. But as man - y as re - ceived, to them he gave the power
C
Am7
G7
C
and His life was the light of men. He came un - to His own,
to be - come the sons of God. But as man - y as re - ceived,
C7
F
C
G7
C
and His own re - ceived Him not, And His life was the light of men.
to them He gave the power to be - come the Sons of God.
CHORUS
C
F
C
Am7
Dm7
In Him was life, in Him was life, and the life was the light of men.
G7
C
C7
F
C
G7
C
In Him was life, in Him was life, and the life was the light of men.

47 If Ye Abide in Me

John 15:7, 16; 16:24

Delinda Bishop

C G7 C7 F
If ye a - bide in me, and my words a - bide in you, ye shall
C G7
ask what ye will, and it shall be done un - to you: Ye have not
3
C G7 C7 F C
chos - en me, but I have chos - en you, and or - dained you, to
G G7 C F
3
go and bear fruit, and that your fruit should re - main: that what so-
C D7
ev - er ye shall ask of the Fa - ther in my name, He may

G G7 C
give it un - to you. Hith-er- to have ye asked no - thing in my name:
F Dm Dm7/G C G7 C
ask,and ye shall re- ceive, shall re - ceive, that your joy may be full.

48 He Hath Shown Thee, O Man

Micah 6:8

Unknown

F C7 F C7 F
He hath shown thee, O man, what is good; and

G7 C7 F F7
what doth the Lord re - quire of thee, but to do just - ly, and to

B♭ B♭m F C7 F
love mer - cy, and to walk hum-bly with Thy God?

49 A New Commandment

John 13:34, 35 Unknown

D Bm G A D
A new com-mand-ment I give un-to you, That you love one an-
Bm G A7 D Bm
oth-er; as I have loved you, That you love one an-oth-er; as
G A7 D D7 G A7 D Bm
Fine
I have loved you. By this shall all men know you are my dis-ci-ples,
G A D D7 G A A7
if you have love one for an-oth-er. By this shall all men know
D Bm Em7 A D
D. C. al Fine
you are my dis-ci-ples, if you have love one for an-oth-er.

50 That I May Know Him

Philippians 3:10

Bess Robertson

F C
That I may know Him, won-der-ful Lord; That I may know him,
F C F
won-der-ful Lord. To know the pow-er of His great re-sur-
C C7
rec-tion and join in fel-low-ship with that of His
F C7 F
suf-fer-ings, and in that be-ing made con-for-ma-ble
B♭ Gm C7 F C7 F
to His death, that I may know Him, won-der-ful Lord.

51 Stand Fast Therefore in the Liberty

Galatians 5:1, 13, 22, 23 — Unknown

Eb (D) Ab (G) F9 (E9)
Stand fast there-fore in the li - ber - ty where-with Christ hath
Bb (A) Ab (G) Bb7 (A7)
made us free, and be not en-tang-led a - gain with the yoke of
Eb (D) Fine Eb(D) (Em) Fm (D°7) Eb°7 Eb (D)
bondage. For, breth-ren, ye have been called un - to li-ber- ty;
Ab (G) F9 (E9) Bb7 (A7) Ab (G)
on - ly use not li - ber - ty for an oc- ca - sion to the
Bb7 (A7) 3 Eb (D) Ab (G)
flesh, but by love serve one an- oth - er. But the fruit of the

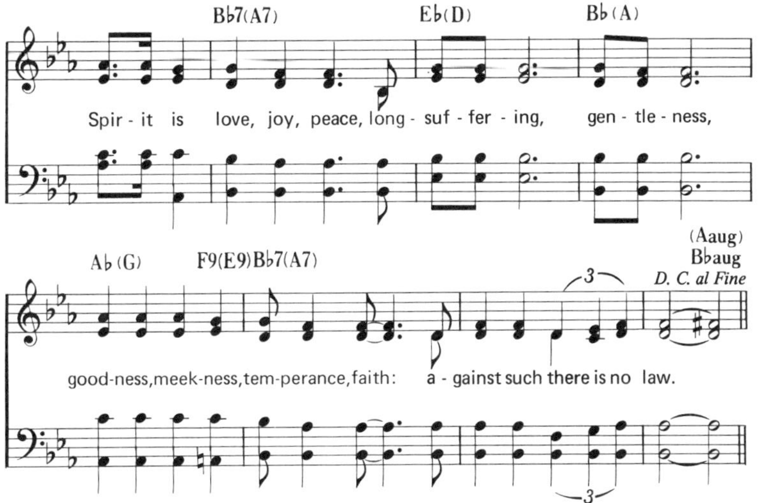
Bb7(A7)
Eb(D)
Bb(A)
Spir - it is love, joy, peace, long - suf - fer - ing, gen - tle - ness,
Ab(G)
F9(E9)Bb7(A7)
(Aaug)
Bbaug
D. C. al Fine
3
good-ness,meek-ness,tem-perance,faith: a - gainst such there is no law.
3

52 Be Filled with the Spirit

Ephesians 5:18, 19 — Unknown

C G7

Be filled with the Spir - it; speak - ing to your - selves in

C

psalms and hymns and spir - i - tual songs, sing - ing and

C7 F G G7 C

mak - ing mel - o - dy in your heart to the Lord.

53 Wherefore God also Hath Highly Exalted Him

Philippians 2:9-11 Elnora Stewart

Eb(D) Ab(G) Eb(D) Bb(A) Eb(D) Bb(A) Eb(D)
Where-fore God al-so hath high-ly ex-alt-ed Him,
Bb7(A7) Eb(D) Bb7(A7) Eb(D)
and giv-en Him a name which is a-bove eve-ry name
(A7)(D)(G) Bb7 Eb Ab Eb(D) Cm(Bm) Ab(G) Eb(D) Bb7(A7) Eb(D)
that at the name of Je-sus eve-ry knee should bow, of
Ab(G) Abm(Gm) Eb(D) (A7) Bb7 Cm(Bm) F7(E7) Bb7(A7)
things in heav'n, and things in earth, and things un-der the earth;
Eb(D) (D) Eb (A7) Bb7 (D7) Eb7 Ab6(G6)
and that eve-ry tongue con-fess that Je-sus Christ is

Fm7 (Em7) Bb A Eb (D) Bb7 (A7) Eb (D)
Lord to the glo - ry of God the Fa - ther.

54 Now unto the King Eternal

1 Timothy 1:17

Lorraine Sonnenberg

F
Now un - to the King e - ter - nal, im - mor - tal, in -

C7 F C7 C7 F C9
vis - i - ble, the on - ly wise God, the on - ly wise God, be

F C7 F
hon - or and glo - ry for ev - er and ev - er. A - men. A -

C7 F C7 F
men. Be hon - or and glo - ry for ev - er and ev - er. A - men.

↑ Indicates entrance of subsequent voices of 4 part round.

55 In Everything Give Thanks

1 Thessalonians 5:18, 16-22
Doyle Brymer
F
C
1. In eve - ry - thing give thanks: for this is the will of God.
2. Re - joice ev - er - more: for this is the will of God.
C7
F
In eve - ry - thing give thanks: for this is the will of God.
Re - joice ev - er - more: for this is the will of God.
F7
In eve - ry - thing give thanks: for this is the will of
Re - joice ev - er more: for this is the will of
Bb
F
C7
1
2
F
F
God in Christ Je - sus con - cern - ing you.
God in Christ Je - sus con - cern - ing you. you.

3. Pray without ceasing . . .
4. Quench not the Spirit . . .
5. Despise not prophesyings . . .
6. Prove all things . . .
7. Hold fast to what is good . . .
8. Abstain from all evil . . .

56 But Ye Are a Chosen Generation

1 Peter 2:9, 10 Unknown

F
Gm
G
But ye are a cho-sen gen-er-a-tion, a roy-al
C
F
priest-hood, an ho-ly na-tion, a pe-cu-liar
Gm
G
C7
peo-ple that ye should show forth the prais-es of Him who has
F
Bb
C7
F
called you out of dark-ness in-to His mar-vel-ous light: which in
Gm
G
C7
F
time past were not a peo-ple, but are now the peo-ple of God.

57 Beloved, Let Us Love One Another

1 John 4:7, 8

Richard Haas

F
C7
Be - lov-ed, let us love one an-oth-er: for
Gm
C
C7
love is of God; and ev - ery one that lov - eth is
F
C7
F
born of God, and know-eth God, he that lov - eth not
F7
Gm
C7
know-eth not God; for God is love. Be - lov-ed,
F
B♭
F
let us love one an - oth-er. First John four sev-en and eight.

58 Thou Art Worthy

Revelation 4:11 Pauline Michael Mills

Bb(A) Eb(D) Bb(A) F(E)
Thou art wor-thy, Thou art wor-thy, Thou art wor-thy, O Lord.
Bb(A) Bb7(A7) Eb(D) Bb(A)
Thou art wor-thy to re-ceive glo-ry, glo-ry and
F7(E7) Bb(A) F(E) Bb(A)
hon-or and pow'r! For Thou hast cre-a-ted, hast all things cre-
F(E) F7(E7) Bb(A)
a-ted, for Thou hast cre-a-ted all things, And for thy
Bb7(A7) Eb(D) Bb(A) F7(E7) Bb(A)
plea-sure they are cre-a-ted; Thou art wor-thy, O Lord.

Index

A new commandment **49**
Ah Lord God! **43**
As for God, His way is perfect **7**
As the hart panteth after the water brooks **18**
Be filled with the Spirit **52**
Be still and know that I am God **25**
Behold! Bless ye the Lord **33**
Beloved, let us love one another **57**
But ye are a chosen generation **56**
Cause me to hear **35**
Come, bless the Lord **34**
Delight thyself also in the Lord **15**
For thou art great **29**
From the rising of the sun **30**
Give unto the Lord **17**
God is not a man **1**
God is our refuge **20**
Great is the Lord **21**
He hath shown thee, O man **48**
He that dwelleth in the secret place **24**
Hear, O Israel **2**
The heavens declare the glory of God **8**
His name is as ointment poured forth **27**
I see the Lord **38**
I waited patiently for the Lord **16**
I will extol Thee, O Lord **12**
I will praise Thee **23**
I will proclaim the greatness of the Lord **3**
I will sing of the mercies **22**
If Thou, O Lord, shouldest mark iniquities **32**
If ye abide in Me **47**
In everything give thanks **55**
In Him was life **46**
Let the beauty of our God **26**
Let us know **44**
The Lord is my light **13**
The Lord will not forsake His people **4**
My glory and the lifter of my head **6**
My soul, wait thou only upon God **19**
Now unto the King eternal **54**
Obey my voice **42**
One thing have I desired **10**
Praise ye the Lord! **36**
Seek ye first **45**
Stand fast therefore in the liberty **51**
The steps of a good man **14**
That I may know Him **50**
Therefore the redeemed of the Lord **41**
Therefore with joy **39**
Thine, O Lord, is the greatness **5**
This is my beloved **37**
This is the day **31**
Thou art worthy **58**
Thou wilt keep him in perfect peace **40**
Thy loving kindness **28**
Unto Thee, O Lord **9**
Wait on the Lord **11**
Wherefore God also hath highly exalted Him **53**